P9-EEJ-077

GEORGE WASHINGTON
A Talk With His Grandchildren

by Dorothy Fay Richards
illustrated by John Nelson

THE CHILD'S WORLD

ELGIN, ILLINOIS 60120

Note: In this story, the author has taken several actual incidents from Washington's life and has narrated them within a fictionalized framework, as if Washington were talking to his grandchildren. The grandchildren were George Washington Custis, who was called Washington, and Eleanor Custis, who was called Nelly. All the events mentioned in this book happened. The author has taken great care to narrate them accurately. The coat was real and did have the holes in it. The letter Washington wrote upon learning that he had been chosen President has been preserved, as has Washington's prayer book. Mrs. Washington did have a parrot, and she often served tea in the afternoon.

President Washington showed great affection toward his grandchildren. But we don't know whether or not he ever told them about these events.

The artist, also, has been careful to be accurate. He worked from portraits of the Washington family and from photos of Mt. Vernon and many objects there.

Library of Congress Cataloging in Publication Data

Richards, Dorothy Fay, 1915-
  George Washington, a talk with his grandchildren.

  SUMMARY: Brief accounts of several incidents in the military career of George Washington.
  1. Washington, George, Pres. U.S., 1732-1799—Juvenile literature. 2. Presidents—United States—Biography—Juvenile literature. [1. Washington, George, Pres. U.S., 1732-1799. 2. Presidents. 3. United States—History—Revolution, 1775-1783]
I. Nelson, John, 1928-   II. Title.
E312.66.R53   973.4'1'0924 [B]   78-8564
ISBN 0-89565-034-7

Distributed by Childrens Press, 1224 West Van Buren Street, Chicago, Illinois 60607.

© 1978 The Child's World, Inc.

It was an April afternoon in 1789. The sun was low in the sky. It was almost time to light the candles. Still, the white-haired man at the desk wrote on — scratch, scratch, scratch — with his quill pen.

"Gentlemen," he wrote, "I have received word today that I have been elected the first President of the United States of America . . ."

The door opened. A girl dressed in pink tiptoed into the room. She was ten years old. She sat down near her grandfather's feet.

George Washington smiled at her.

"A story, perhaps?" she asked.

"Is it that time already, Nelly? Where did the day go? Well, never mind. Which story do you want?"

"The dog!"

The General threw back his head and laughed. "Oh, all right, Nelly. But you always ask for that one!

"As you know, it happened when we Americans were fighting the English. It was at Germantown. The battle was going very well for us. And then, all of a sudden, it wasn't! So we started to pull back.

"Suddenly, in the middle of all the fighting, there came . . . a dog! He was running away from the English, who were winning. He was joining us, even though we were losing! He followed us all the way to camp.

"One of the soldiers saw that the dog was wearing a collar. He found out that the dog belonged to General Howe! And Howe was the general we were fighting!

"The next day, we decided to return the dog. Our soldiers thought it was funny that the General's dog had come to us. And they thought it was even funnier to return him. How they laughed!

"Two men carried a white flag. They took the dog across to General Howe's camp. The white flag

meant, 'Don't shoot. We have a message.' The men shouted as loudly as they could, 'General Washington returning General Howe's dog.' It was good to have something to laugh at that day!"

Nelly had heard the story many times. But she still laughed when her grandfather told it.

Now the library door opened again. A boy, eight years old, came in. He carried a coat. The coat had been part of a uniform.

"Grandfather, I found this just now. Grandmother said you might tell Nelly and me what it is. Will you, sir?"

"Well, Washington, as you can see, it is an old coat. But did you see those holes? Here, and here?"

"And here and here, also. What made them?"

"Musket balls. It happened in a battle long ago. I was very young. I had not even married your grandmother yet. Back then, this country was new. It was not called the United States.

"Three different nations said, 'It's mine!' The Indians, who lived here, were one. The French, who had explored part of it, were another. And the English, who had built towns in part of it, were the third.

"Well, the French and the Indians paired up to-
gether. They tried to drive the English out. I was
helping the English. My job was to advise the English
general. I said, 'Sir, the French and Indians won't
fight you in the open. They will hide behind trees. It
will be a different kind of battle from any you have
seen!'

"But the English general could not change his way
of doing things. 'There is only one way to fight,' he
said. 'Head on! Out in the open! That's how we will
fight!'

"So down the road came the English in their bright red coats. They marched in straight lines. I was with them. And, sure enough, the French and Indians were hidden. They shot down the English as they marched. The English could not see them. They could not fight back.

"Two horses were shot from under me that day. I was wearing that coat. And I got the holes you see. But I wasn't hurt."

"Grandfather," said Nelly, "that coat has a Christmas ribbon in its pocket. What is it for?"

"That ribbon is to remind me of Trenton," said the white-haired man. "The battle at Trenton happened at Christmas time. You know, children, we have talked about two wars. In the first war, I fought with the English. I got the holes in the coat in that war.

"Later, there was a second war. In it, we—the Americans—fought against the English."

"Is that the war the dog was in?" asked Nelly.

Her grandfather laughed. "Yes."

"Why did we have a second war?" asked his grandson.

"America used to belong to England," said the General. "But we wanted to have our own country. We wanted to be free. We didn't want a king. And we didn't want the English to tell us what to do. To become free, we had to fight the English.

"It was a long, hard war. At first, it seemed as though we were going to lose. But we thought, Maybe we can turn things around if we can win at Trenton. And we can win if we can surprise the enemy.

" 'The day after Christmas, we'll attack!' we said. 'We'll be there early in the morning, right at dawn.'

"You see, usually soldiers celebrate on Christmas night. Then they sleep soundly the next morning. Because of this, we knew the enemy would not expect an attack.

"About four in the afternoon, on Christmas day, we started out. In freezing weather, we marched to the places where boats and barges were hidden. The men shivered in the biting wind. How they worked to get horses and cannons safely onto the huge barges.

"We had to take men and horses and cannons across the freezing Delaware River. By now, it was dark.

"We made many trips back and forth across the river. The wind was blowing and biting. Soon, it was raining and sleeting too. We wanted to have all the men across by midnight. But it took until half-past three in the morning. And it took another hour to get ready to march.

"I sent General Sullivan by the river road to Trenton. General Greene and I took the upper road. We had nine miles to march.

"Daylight came, and still we had not reached the town. The rain and sleet had turned to snow. As we got near, I heard bugle calls. They were waking up the enemy!

"But . . . praise be! I also heard cannon fire. That meant General Sullivan was entering the town. We had done it! We were attacking at dawn!

"Enemy soldiers tumbled from their beds. But it was too late. Very soon, their white flag was flying. They had given up!

"Because of that battle, American people began to believe we would win the war. It was still a long time till peace came. But our hope was high after that day.

"I felt thankful that night. My heart was full when I prayed to God."

Now the door opened once more. This time, some-
one was carrying a candle into the room. It was Mrs.
Washington. "Tea in a few minutes," she said. She
set the candle on the desk. Quietly, she left the room.

"Sir, did you still wear this coat when you were fighting the English?" Washington asked.

"No. But its tatters and holes remind me of the poor rags many of our soldiers had to wear. I shall always keep it."

Nelly's eyes were wide. "Sir, why did your soldiers wear poor rags?"

U. S. 2019995

"There was no money to buy uniforms, Nelly. The soldiers' clothes got all ragged. During the winters, I even had to borrow blankets. I got them from people in near-by villages. The men wore the blankets around them. That's all that kept them from freezing.

"Look in this pocket. What do you find?"

"A pair of knitting needles! That's a funny thing to find in your old coat!"

"They are there to remind you, and me, and anyone else who finds them, of the good deed your grandmother did."

"Grandmother? What did she do, sir?"

"At Valley Forge, she came to stay through the winters with me. Many of the soldiers had no shoes. Their feet and ankles were wrapped in rags. When they walked in the snow, their footprints were marked with blood.

"When your grandmother saw this, she knitted socks for them! Other officers' wives saw her doing it, and they joined in. Her idea of socks really helped. Her hands were never still.

"But, of course, everyone was busy at Valley Forge. It's a wonder we lived through those times. Some weeks there was no meat. Sometimes, there was hardly any food at all!"

"Grandfather, what is this little book in the other pocket?"

"That is my own book of prayers, Nelly. I am glad you found it. I wrote each prayer out in my best handwriting when I was twenty years old. And I carry the words in my mind.

"Many times I have prayed them. I prayed them in the snow at Valley Forge and while crossing the Delaware River."

General Washington stood up, straight and tall. He picked up the candlestick. "Come, Washington. Come, Nelly. Your grandmother will never bring out the old coat again if we don't hurry. Didn't she say tea was about ready?"

They hurried to the parlor. Mrs. Washington's parrot turned her head and glared at them. "About time! About time!" she squawked.